Solar ENERGY

David and Patricia Armentrout

rourkeeducationalmedia.com

www.rourkeeducationalmedia.com

PHOTO CREDITS: © Thomas Gordon: page 4; © Mehmet Salih Guler: page 5; © Kapu: page 7 background; © tomos3: page 6 left; © Andrew Penner: page 7 top; © Hugo de Wolf: page 7 bottom; © SOHO Consortium: page 9; © Jirijura: page 10; Courtesy: NASA: page 12, 13, 39; © PhotoDisc: page 15; © StillFX: page 17; © Giorgio Fochesato: page 19; © Oktay Ortakcioglu: page 20; © Duncan Gilbert: page 21; © Tobias Machhaus: page 25; © Sergei Butorin: page 25 inset; © Markus Gann: page 26; © ConstantGardener: page 27; © Otmar Smit: page 29; Courtesy: Sandia/Photo by Randy Montoya: page 30, 33; © Seimans: page 31; © Marli Miller: page 32; © Eliza Snow: page 34; © Kativ: page 35; Courtesy: Panasonic World Solar Challenge: page 37; Courtesy: United States Air Force/ Senior Airman Larry E. Reid Jr.: page 43

Edited by Kelli Hicks

Cover design by Nicky Stratford, bdpublishing.com
Interior design by Teri Intzegian

Library of Congress Cataloging-in-Publication Data

Armentrout, David and Patricia
  Solar Energy / David and Patricia Armentrout.
      p. cm. -- (Let's Explore Global Energy)
Summary: Introduces Solar Energy and its positive or negative impact on the environment, particularly our future.
  Includes index.
  ISBN 978-1-60472-325-0 (Hardcover)
  ISBN 978-1-61741-540-1 (Softcover)
  1. Solar Energy--Juvenile literature. I. Title.

Rourke Educational Media
Printed in the United States of America,
North Mankato, Minnesota

rourkeeducationalmedia.com

customerservice@rourkeeducationalmedia.com • PO Box 643328 Vero Beach, Florida 32964

Table of Contents

CHAPTER ONE

Energy

Do you know what energy is? Scientists define energy as the ability to do work. That makes sense, because when you have a lot of energy, you feel like you can do many things. You might even say, "I have so much energy I feel like I could run 20 miles." Running is work, and you would certainly need energy to run 20 miles. How does your body get energy? It comes from food. Food is the fuel your body converts to energy.

Just as our bodies convert chemicals from food to energy, we convert some of Earth's resources, like coal and oil, into energy products like electricity and fuels. We use these products to heat and light our homes, schools, and businesses, and to power our cars and other machines.

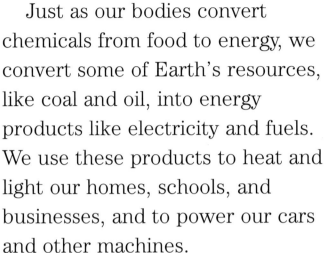

Fuel for Thought

Physics is a science that deals with energy. Physicists study all kinds of energy including chemical energy, the kind of energy found in food that your body stores before you put it to good use.

Fuel for Thought

Coal, oil, and natural gas are fossil fuels. They formed from plants and animals that lived millions of years ago. Coal formed over time when plant remains compressed underground with soil, clay, and minerals. Oil and natural gas formed long ago when tiny sea animals and plants died and sank to the seabed. Bacteria, heat, soil, and pressure slowly transformed the dead matter into oil and gas.

Coal

Oil

Fossil Fuels

Natural Gas

CHAPTER TWO

Solar Energy

We cannot create energy, but we can convert one form of energy to another and make that energy work for us. Solar energy, or energy from the Sun, is one example.

The Sun is our ultimate source of energy. The Sun is responsible for all energy. The energy that keeps the Sun burning day after day is the same energy that controls our weather and supports life on Earth.

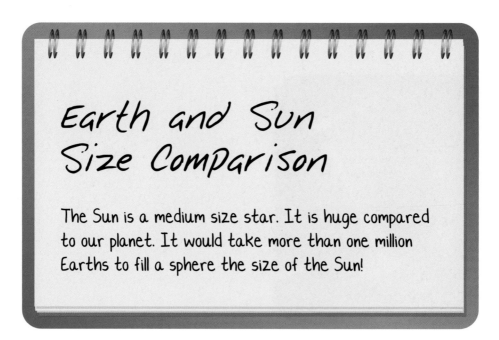

Earth and Sun Size Comparison

The Sun is a medium size star. It is huge compared to our planet. It would take more than one million Earths to fill a sphere the size of the Sun!

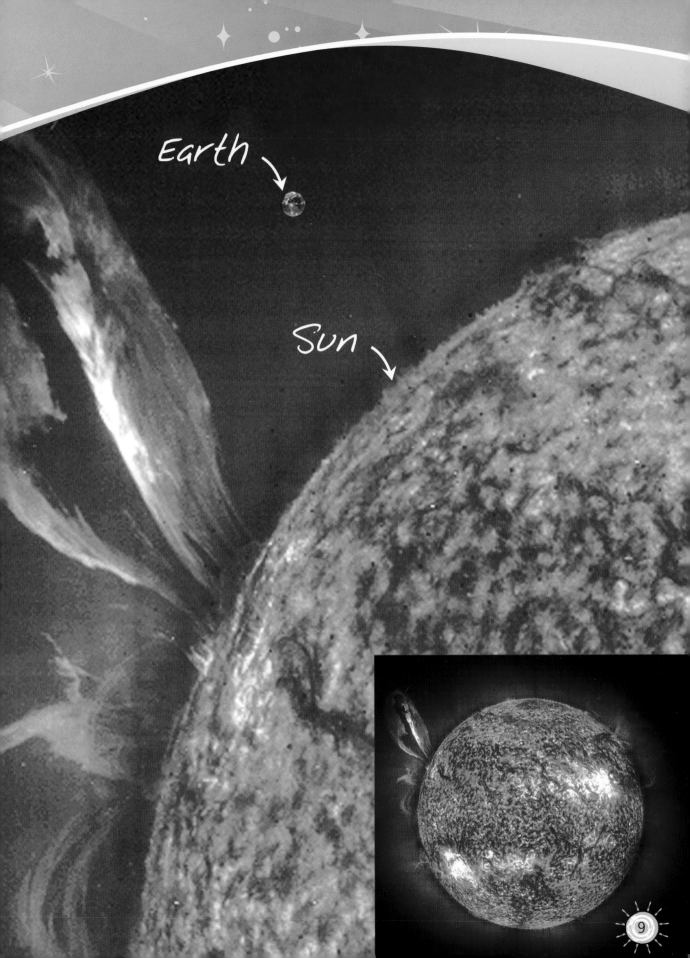

Earth

Sun

When you stand outside on a hot summer day, it is clear the Sun provides heat energy. When you look around and see green grass, blue sky, and a rainbow of colorful flowers, it's clear the Sun provides light energy. You might wonder, though, how the Sun is responsible for all energy. Let's explore more about the Sun and solar energy.

CHAPTER THREE

What makes up the Sun?

Several chemical elements make up the Sun. About 74 percent of the Sun is **hydrogen** gas and about 25 percent is **helium** gas. Other elements including **oxygen** make up the rest. The Sun's center, or core, is more dense, or heavier, than its outer layers.

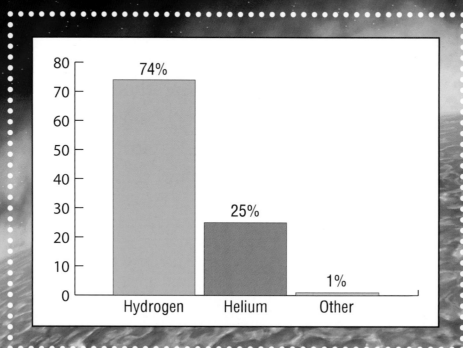

Extreme heat and pressure in the core changes hydrogen to helium. The result is a constant massive release of energy. The process is **nuclear fusion**.

Fuel for Thought ⚡

Everything in the universe, including our Sun, is made of tiny atoms. Atoms contain even smaller particles of protons and electrons that carry an electric charge.

CHAPTER FOUR

Where does the Sun's Energy Go?

Energy from the Sun leaves the core and cools as it passes through the outer layers of gas. The energy, in the form of heat and light, enters space in every direction. It takes just over eight minutes for sunlight (solar energy) to travel 93 million miles and reach Earth!

Since sunlight travels in all directions, only a fraction of the Sun's energy reaches Earth's **atmosphere**. Some of the energy bounces off Earth and back into space. Much of it is absorbed and converted to heat. Plants store a small amount of solar energy in their cells. What plants do with the solar energy makes nearly all life on Earth possible.

CHAPTER FIVE

Plants and Solar Energy

When the Sun shines, plant cells take action! They transform solar energy to chemical energy by **photosynthesis**. During photosynthesis, plant cells absorb sunlight and carbon dioxide from the air. At the same time, plant cells remove oxygen from water and release it into the air. The process produces sugars and starches that are either stored or used as food for the plant.

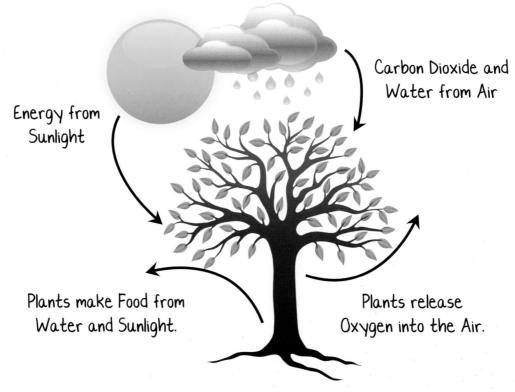

Carbon Dioxide and
Water from Air

Energy from
Sunlight

Plants make Food from
Water and Sunlight.

Plants release
Oxygen into the Air.

Fuel for Thought ⚡

Animals that lived millions of years ago ate plants, or ate animals that ate plants. Their bodies stored chemical energy from the plants. After the plants and animals died, their chemical energy slowly turned into chemical energy in fossil fuels. Wow! That means solar energy absorbed by plants millions of years ago indirectly fuels our cars and heats our homes today!

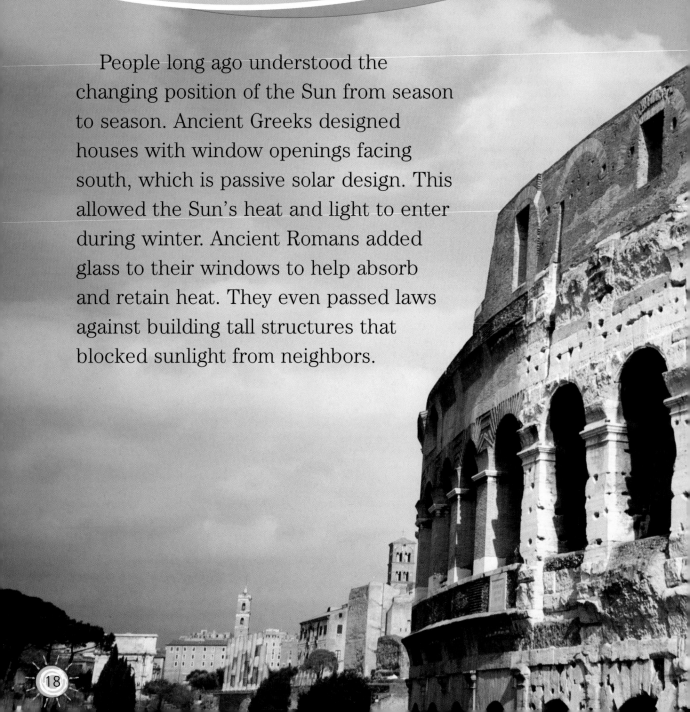

CHAPTER SIX

Early uses of Solar Energy

People long ago understood the changing position of the Sun from season to season. Ancient Greeks designed houses with window openings facing south, which is passive solar design. This allowed the Sun's heat and light to enter during winter. Ancient Romans added glass to their windows to help absorb and retain heat. They even passed laws against building tall structures that blocked sunlight from neighbors.

The Anasazi cliff dwellers were the ancestors of Pueblo Indians. They built energy **efficient** homes in the Southwest. The Anasazi carved their homes in south-facing cliffs that had large rock overhangs. During the summer, when the Sun's angle was high in the sky, their homes stayed cool from the shade of the overhang. In winter, when the Sun was low, their homes bathed in heat and light energy.

People long ago also used the Sun's heat energy to dry clothes, crops, and animal skins. We still use the Sun's energy for these things today.

CHAPTER SEVEN

Global Energy Sources

Renewable Energy

SOLAR ENERGY

- Heat and light energy from the Sun
- Renews day after day as the Sun shines

WIND ENERGY

- Motion energy from the wind
- Renews day after day as the wind blows

HYDROPOWER ENERGY

- Energy from moving water
- Renews day after day in waves and flowing rivers

GEOTHERMAL ENERGY

- Heat and steam energy beneath the Earth's surface

BIOMASS ENERGY

- Plant material and animal waste used to generate energy

Some energy sources, such as fossil fuels, take a long time to replenish. They are nonrenewable energy sources. Renewable sources, such as sunlight, replenish in a relatively short time. Listed below are examples of renewable and nonrenewable energy sources.

Non-Renewable Energy

COAL
- Solid that takes millions of years to form
- Mined from the Earth

OIL
- Liquid that takes millions of years to form
- Pumped from the ground

NATURAL GAS
- Colorless odorless gas that takes millions of years to form
- Pumped from the ground

PROPANE GAS
- Natural gas that becomes a liquid gas at high pressure or at low temperature
- Found with natural gas and oil

NUCLEAR ENERGY
- Stored in atoms-the smallest particles of chemical elements
- Formed using uranium ore which is mined from the earth

CHAPTER EIGHT

Solar Energy Today

For the last 200 years the world has relied on fossil fuels for its primary energy needs. However, fossil fuel supplies are limited. Some experts believe oil production will last only 35 years, while coal production may last 200 years. The Sun comes up every day. It is a free, renewable, and nonpolluting energy source. It is important to look at all these factors, because the world's energy needs grow as **industry** and population grows. Fortunately, **technology** has improved the way we collect and store sunlight and how we use it as a global energy.

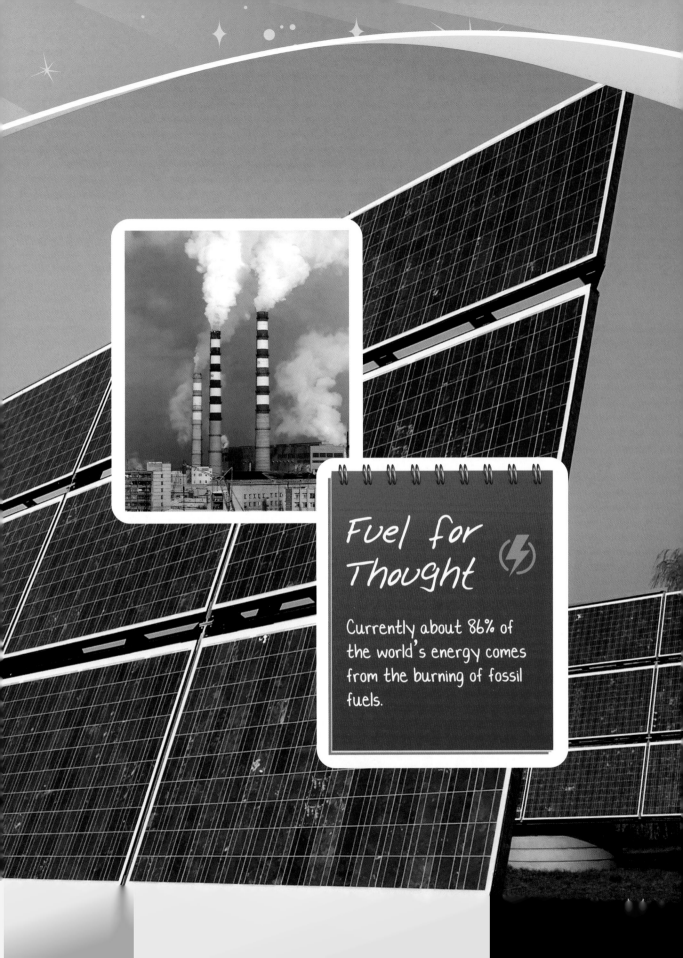

Fuel for Thought ⚡

Currently about 86% of the world's energy comes from the burning of fossil fuels.

CHAPTER NINE

Solar Thermal Collectors

Thermal flat-plate collectors collect solar energy. You may have noticed some homes and businesses with them on the rooftops. Thermal collectors absorb heat energy, also called thermal energy, from the Sun. They transfer it somewhere else to perform work. The collectors work well for heating water for swimming pools and hot water heaters.

Greenhouses are solar collectors too. Plants grow well inside them because their glass or plastic walls keep thermal energy inside, even when it's cold outside. Greenhouses allow us to control the environment in which plants grow. They protect plants from harsh winds, heavy rains, and even blizzards. We control the amount of water plants get too, through irrigation systems.

We use greenhouses to grow many plants year round, including house and garden plants, herbs and vegetables, and flowers and trees. Farmers sow seeds in greenhouses in the dead of winter, so by spring, plants are ready for sale, or for planting in traditional farms. Greenhouses are especially important for the produce industry. Grocery stores carry typical summer vegetables, like tomatoes, because farmers grow them year round in greenhouses.

A basic flat-plate collector uses a metal plate with a special black coating to absorb heat. The plate lies inside an **insulated** box covered with clear glass. Water-filled pipes run through the box to a storage tank. When sunlight passes through the glass, it heats the water in the pipes, which transfers to the storage tank. With this system, the water that flows through the pipes is the same water used for bathing and laundry.

A **parabolic trough** is also a solar thermal collector. It is a long, curved shiny panel, or mirror. Solar thermal power plants use rows and rows of them. Trough collectors direct sunlight to tubes that run down the center of the troughs. A liquid, such as oil, flows through the tubes and transfers heat to produce steam. Solar thermal power plants use steam to drive the blades of a **turbine**. The turbine transfers energy to a **generator**, which produces electricity.

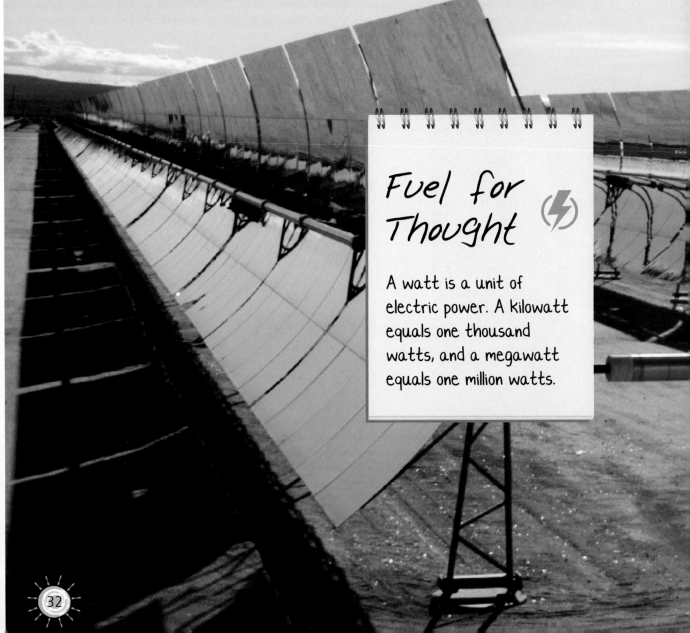

California's Mojave Desert is home to Solar Generating Energy Systems, a group of seven solar thermal power plants. They use the parabolic trough design, along with natural gas, to produce electricity. Together the plants can produce 310 megawatts of power, enough for 230,000 homes. Currently they make up the largest solar power complex in the world.

Fuel for Thought

A watt is a unit of electric power. A kilowatt equals one thousand watts, and a megawatt equals one million watts.

A solar power tower is another solar thermal power plant design. Thousands of flat, moveable mirrors called heliostats surround a tower. The heliostats direct sunlight to the top of the tower where tubes filled with liquid sodium collect the solar heat. Liquid sodium gets very hot, at least 1200 degrees Fahrenheit (649 degrees Celsius). The salty liquid holds heat better than water or oil. The heat produces steam for electricity, or it is stored and used later when there is no sunshine.

CHAPTER TEN

Solar Cells

Photovoltaic (PV) **cells**, or solar cells, convert sunlight directly to electricity. PV cells are thin discs made of chemical elements such as **silicon**. When tiny elements in sunlight called photons hit the chemical elements in the solar cells, they create an electric current.

When a group of PV cells are wired together, it is called a solar module, or panel. A solar array is two or more panels wired together. A single PV cell can power something small like a calculator. Several panels can generate electricity for many things, like homes, schools, and even space satellites.

CHAPTER ELEVEN

Making Solar Cells Better

An American inventor built the first working solar cell in the 1880s. It was about one percent efficient. That means only one percent of the absorbed solar energy generated electricity. Since then, researchers have made solar energy production cheaper and more efficient.

Solar Vehicles

Solar cars are electric vehicles. They use solar cells to convert sunlight to electricity. The electricity is stored in battery packs. A solar car looks futuristic. Many look like solar panels on wheels! That's because in order to generate enough power, a solar car's surface has to be covered with photovoltaic cells.

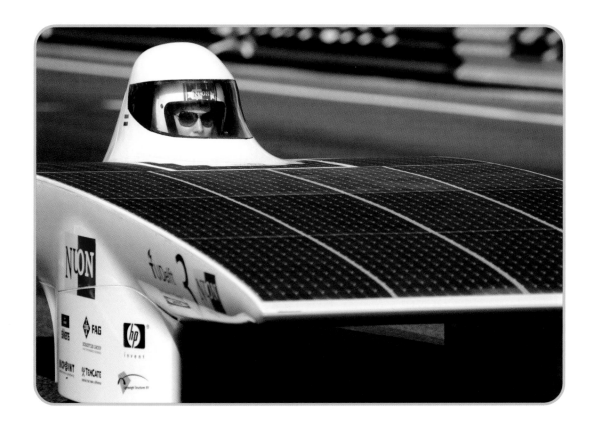

Unfortunately, solar cars are not ready to replace gas-powered vehicles. Solar cell efficiency limits their usefulness as transportation vehicles. Engineers and hobbyists build most solar cars to compete in speed and distance races around the world. To make cars as efficient as possible, they eliminate extra space and weight. The interiors usually have just enough room for a driver to squeeze in. The competitions promote solar technology and encourage builders to improve their machines.

Solar Aircraft

Imagine an aircraft that could soar through the sky all day without landing to refuel. Some scientists hope that eventually solar aircraft will be able to do just that. For now, solar airplanes are experimental. Solar airplanes, like solar cars, are electric vehicles. Solar panels cover the plane's upper surface and capture sunlight. The panels convert solar energy to electricity and store it in batteries.

Helios was one of several unmanned solar aircraft built by NASA (National Aeronautics and Space Administration). Engineers designed it to fly high and to stay aloft for long periods. Operators flew and managed it by remote control from a ground station. The Helios was 247 feet (75.2 meters) from tip to tip, longer than the wingspan of a Boeing 747 jumbo jet. Helios set several flight records, including the highest flight for an unmanned aircraft. Unfortunately, it broke up during a test flight and crashed into the Pacific Ocean.

Fuel for Thought ⚡

The Gossamer Penguin was the first piloted solar aircraft. It traveled just under two miles in 1980 when its pilot completed a public demonstration flight.

CHAPTER TWELVE

Solar Energy Advantages and Disadvantages

With advancements in technology, you might think solar energy is a simple solution for the world's increasing need for energy. Unfortunately, it is not simple. Solar energy production has advantages and disadvantages, just like energy production from other sources.

While sunlight is free, the cost of collecting and converting it to a useable energy is not. Cost is one factor people look at when they consider solar energy. The columns to the right list some solar energy advantages and disadvantages. Can you think of more?

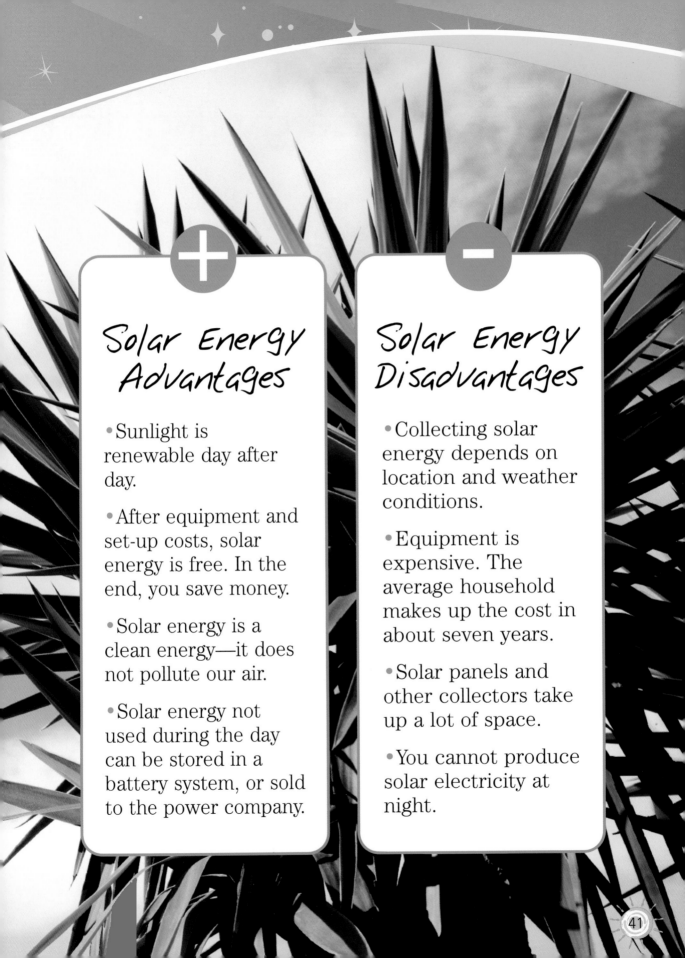

Solar Energy Advantages

- Sunlight is renewable day after day.

- After equipment and set-up costs, solar energy is free. In the end, you save money.

- Solar energy is a clean energy—it does not pollute our air.

- Solar energy not used during the day can be stored in a battery system, or sold to the power company.

Solar Energy Disadvantages

- Collecting solar energy depends on location and weather conditions.

- Equipment is expensive. The average household makes up the cost in about seven years.

- Solar panels and other collectors take up a lot of space.

- You cannot produce solar electricity at night.

CHAPTER THIRTEEN

Can Solar Energy Brighten our Future?

When we enter a dark room, we flip a switch to turn on the lights without a second thought. When the power goes out, we quickly realize how much we depend on electricity. Is solar energy a good source for electricity? In many places, it is. Solar thermal and PV plants generate electricity around the world. Several large PV plants operate in Europe. Nellis Air Force Base in Nevada operates the largest PV plant in the United States. It uses 70,000 solar panels to create electricity. Plans for new solar power plants are in the works worldwide.

Experts believe solar energy has the ability to work for more of us. However, we need to increase efficiency and reduce the costs of generating electricity from solar energy. With continued research, solar energy could help brighten our future.

CHAPTER FOURTEEN

Solar Timeline

Use the solar timeline to learn some interesting facts about solar technology.

4.54 Billion Years Ago
The Earth forms and begins to absorb energy from the Sun.

7th Century BC
People use simple magnifying glasses to concentrate sunlight and make fire.

5th Century BC
Greeks use passive solar housing design.

1st Century AD
Romans use a form of glass in window openings to retain the Sun's heat.

6th Century AD
Roman laws prohibit tall buildings that block sunlight.

13th Century AD
Anasazi people build south-facing cliff homes. Italians build modern greenhouses.

1767
Swiss scientist Horace de Saussure builds the world's first solar collector.

1800s
A period of solar thermal and photovoltaic advancement begins.

1883
American inventor Charles Fritts develops a working solar cell.

1905

Albert Einstein publishes a paper on the photoelectric effect with his theory of relativity and later receives the Nobel Prize for his efforts.

1920s

California and Florida homes use flat-plate thermal collectors for water heating.

1954

U.S. researchers at Bell Labs develop six percent efficient silicon solar cells.

1958

The U.S. launches the first spacecraft with solar panels—satellite Vanguard 1.

1973

Solar cells power U.S. Space Station Skylab.

1977

Operation of the Solar Energy Research Institute, now the National Renewable Energy Laboratory (NREL) begins in Boulder, Colorado. The United States Department of Energy forms. President Carter installs solar panels on the White House.

1980

American physicist and inventor Paul MacCready builds Solar Challenger—the first piloted solar-powered aircraft.

1987

The first biannual solar car race—World Solar Challenge—takes place in Australia.

1993

The NREL's Solar Energy Research Facility is established.

2002

President George W. Bush installs two solar water-heating systems at the White House.

2007

Solar cell efficiency exceeds 40 percent.

Glossary

atmosphere (AT-muhs-fear): a mix of gases that surround a planet

efficient (uh-FISH-uhnt): working without wasting energy

generator (JEN-uh-ray-ter): a machine that converts energy to electricity

helium (HEE-lee-um): a light colorless gas that does not burn

hydrogen (HYE-druh-juhn): a colorless gas that does burn

industry (IN-dus-tree): manufacturing companies and other business

insulated (IN-suh-layt-ed): having material to prevent the loss of heat

nuclear fusion (NOO-klee-ur-FYOO-zhuhn): energy created when atom particles join

oxygen (OK-suh-juhn): a colorless gas found in air

parabolic trough (par-eh-BAH-lik-trawf): a long, narrow bowl-shaped container

photosynthesis (FOE-toe-SIN-thuh-siss): a chemical process by which plants make their food

photovoltaic cells (FOE-toe-vol-TAY-ik-sells): devices that can produce electricity when exposed to sunlight

silicon (SIL-uh-kuhn): a chemical element found in sand

technology (tek-NOL-uh-jee): using science and skills to improve upon things

turbine (TUR-bine): an engine driven by air, water, steam, or gas

Index

Further Reading

Morris, Neil. *Solar Power*. Smart Apple Media, 2006.

Thomas, Isabel. *The Pros and Cons of Solar Power*. Rosen Central, 2007.

Walker, Niki. *Harnessing Power from the Sun*. Crabtree Publishing, 2007.

Websites to Visit

www.doe.gov/forstudentsandkids.htm

http://www.solarenergy.org/resources/youngkids.html

http://powerhousekids.com

About the Authors

David and Patricia Armentrout specialize in nonfiction children's books. They enjoy exploring different topics and have written about many subjects, including sports, animals, history, and people. David and Patricia love to spend their free time outdoors with their two boys and dog Max.